Walking With God

STAN HUBERFELD

Walking With God

Stan Huberfeld

Copyright 2008

H.G. Publishing

Langhorne, Pennsylvania 19047

Library of Congress Control Number: 2007941987

ISBN 978-0-9801037-0-0

Steps on the Walk

Forward

First and foremost, I need to say thank you to Jesus (Yeshua Ben Josef), my Lord, Savior and Best Friend. All that I am, all that I have, is a gift from You.

I am a well educated man. I have served in the U.S. Army. I have played many sports throughout my life. I have started a few businesses (some even made money), and owned multiple properties. I have traveled to more places than most. Still, life was empty and made no real sense.

It was not until I entered into a personal relationship with God, through Jesus Christ, that I understood the meaning of life. Through this relationship there is meaning to every day, every moment of my walk on this planet. In addition, I know for sure where I will be 100 years from now and beyond.

My blessings include my beautiful wife, Deborah, two great kids – Sara and Jesse – and the peace and joy in my heart that can only come from God.

Introduction

I have assembled some of the events in my life as they relate to God. There is a common thread in each of the stories. All I did was show up and seek to be obedient to His Word (The Bible) and His Spirit. He does all the rest. It is not about religion. It is about relationship.

It is my hope that as I share some of the stories of how God has blessed me, you are encouraged to begin a life with Him as Lord, Savior and Best Friend. If you have already made that decision, then be encouraged to walk more closely with Him.

Loving Me Right Where I Was

God loves me, and that love is and has been a constant. Since March 15, 1984, my day of commitment, everything has changed from my perspective.

In 1979, I met a man named Boyd. Boyd was the public relations manager of a dairy cooperative and the purchaser of printed materials (brochures, annual reports, etc.) for the organization. I was the owner of a printing company, and so the Lord brought us together. Boyd's life was about as different from mine as two peoples' lives could be. He was a committed Christian, lay pastor, farm boy, retired Air Force officer, and one who really did not embrace sports or worldly values. I, on the other hand, am Jewish, love all sports having played many, was money-focused, an alcoholic, drug user, gambler and party animal. Boyd knew all of this about me and always expressed a sincere interest in my life. What I was doing, whom I did it with, how and why. He was never judgmental.

One day, he and I went to lunch at a nearby restaurant. When the waitress approached, she asked if we would like a cocktail with our meal. I replied first and said "sure, I'll have a Heineken." Boyd's response was to say that he didn't care for an alcoholic beverage because it was contrary to his faith. Being the good salesman, I told the waitress to forget my beer and make it a cold water. Boyd interjected, "No, you want a beer so have a beer." You see, what he was doing had nothing to do with beer and everything to do with love.

As our lunch proceeded, I asked Boyd to explain his faith in detail, leaving out nothing. You see, I knew about Jews, Catholics and Protestants. My experiences were that they were really very similar, less the sign out front and a few rituals. Boyd's answer was quite different. He knew God personally through the sacrifice of Jesus at Calvary. That sacrifice was God's personal gift, and Boyd accepted it fully in his heart. As a result, he allowed God to reign in all parts of his life. The Bible is God's inerrant word to us, and the Trinity is the oneness (*echaud*) of God.

Although I saw and appreciated the depth of his belief, I could only partially understand. Two weeks later, Boyd, 52 years of age and in great health, died. I was staggered, to say the least. I went to his funeral in a small town, Cochranville, PA and was deeply moved by testimonies shared by dozens of people of how Boyd touched their lives. As I drove home on the turnpike, all I could think about was how Boyd always said: "When it comes to God, tell Him exactly what is in your mind and heart. Hold back nothing. Then, remember to give Him equal time. The only place you are going to find out what God has to say is in the Bible."

So here I was, 33 years old, and I was setting out to buy my first Bible at the local bookstore. With much excitement, I was directed to Aisle #6 to make my purchase. When I arrived at the section, I was surprised to find so many translations — none of which I was able to identify with. Where was the Gideon when I needed it? It was always in hotel rooms! As I pondered my decision, I saw one Bible that was a parallel study edition (four translations in one book). With four translations, I figured *one* of them had to be correct, so I made my purchase. For the next two years, I read my Bible regularly and took Sunday morning walks in the woods with my dog, talking to God.

During those 2 years, I discovered that my insurance agent, Steve, was a man of Christian faith. Once again, God had gone before me. As Steve learned of my relationship with Boyd and my Bible reading, he offered himself as a resource for questions and counsel. On March 15, 1984, Steve and I were having breakfast in King of Prussia, PA to review the annual insurance needs of the printing company.

After the business portion of the time had expired, he challenged me with a question: "What is standing between what you believe today and fully embracing the Bible, just as it is?" This included opening the door to my heart and asking Jesus to come in and be my personal Lord, Savior and best friend. I offered half a dozen items to which I objected. The rest of the Bible, I believed.

"Okay," he said. "Let's take those six or so items and let's move them aside for now. Out of the remaining hundreds of things, pick one and prove to me that it is true!"

"I can't," I said. "I just choose to believe it." "Fine," he responded. "Can we call that belief faith?" I replied that "faith" was a fair word to use. Then came the close.

"Let's take back the six or so items you do not believe and cover them with the same faith that you are already using for the rest of the Bible, none of which you can prove is true," he said. "Because it's either all true or none of it is true. If everyone took out the 1% he doesn't agree with, where would the oneness (*echaud*) of God be? Everyone would have his own God."

This all made sense to me, yet I was not about to be hooked by some slick-talking insurance agent! As we parted company, he encouraged me to embrace it all or forget it all.

While driving down the highway (US Route 202 North), I threw it up to God in prayer. "Well God, is it true or not?" The answer came in a wave of peace that covered my heart and my whole being. While sitting at a red light at the corner of Allendale Road and Route 202, I said this simple prayer: "Lord, I know I am a sinner. I believe that Jesus died as payment for my sins past, present and future. Thank you that by His shed blood at the cross, I am forgiven. Please come into my heart to be my Lord, Savior and best Friend."

At that moment, my name was inscribed in the Lamb's Book of Life (the book containing the names of those who are to be in heaven) for eternity.

Visited by an Angel

Some years prior to 1984, perhaps around 1981, a unique event took place in my life. The time was early evening, around 8:00 p.m. It was the dead of winter and a huge snowstorm was taking place, so I was hunkered down for the night with my trusty side-kick, Behn (a coonhound-Springer spaniel mixed breed dog).

The evening was interrupted by a knock at my front door. When I answered it, there stood an attractive, well-dressed young woman! With the wind howling and snow blowing, she explained that her car had skidded off the road on Bridgetown Pike and she needed to use a phone to call her dad. I invited her in and offered my phone. The first strange part of this visit was that my dog, which was very aggressive when strangers first came to the door but friendly once they were allowed inside, never barked at all.

The young lady used the phone and said there was no answer, so perhaps the lines were down. She asked if she could stay awhile and warm herself, as she was not properly dressed for the blizzard we were having. "Of course," I replied, offering her some warm, dry sweats to change into, which she accepted. As we sat by my fireplace, I asked her why she chose my house, since I lived in a court of two rows of 6 homes. "Your house was the only one with lights on," she said. That seemed strange to me. However, I couldn't see my neighbors' homes from my windows, and I wasn't about to go outside to verify it. Over the next few hours we shared the warmth of the fire and personal conversation, along with drinks and snacks. Every half-hour she would attempt to call her dad, and returned with the same comment – "No answer."

After a few hours, she returned from one of these attempts and said her call had gone through, and that her dad would be here in about 15 minutes. She changed back into her professional clothing while I answered the knock that signaled her dad had arrived. Again, strangely, Behn did not bark. We exchanged parting pleasantries and the two of them walked down my driveway. I stood in the foyer for about 15 seconds after closing my door. Something was just weird. Not unpleasant, just weird. I walked outside and down the driveway after them. From that vantage point, I could see the road for about a half-mile. I saw nothing. In just those few seconds between the time they left and the time I followed, they were gone. There were no tire tracks in the snow on the street. There were no automobile headlights anywhere. There was just nothing. The only sound was the howling wind. I remember standing there in the storm for those few moments in disbelief, then returning to the warmth of my house.

At this point in my life, I was living in spiritual darkness, so I just wrote the event off to WOW and had another beer. In later years I was to become aware of who God really is and what His nature really is. I believe that I was visited by angels, pure and simple. When I get to heaven I will find out the rest of the details (Hebrews 13:2). And that is O.K.

God Shows Himself to an Unbeliever

It was mid-April, 1984 and the time to begin spring's chores. I was living in a townhouse in the middle of a row of 6 units. So, I set out to mow my small lawn and neaten up the property. While mowing the rear lawn, I accidentally aroused some ground wasps. One of them took great exception to my actions. It flew right at my face and stung me in the corner of my eye. As I let go of the lawn mower, it flew at my face and stung me a second time in the same area. At that moment, I abandoned the scene and ran around the row of homes to my front door. En route, I passed my neighbor, a non-believer. She looked up from her gardening and exclaimed "Oh my goodness! What has happened to your eye?" I told her what had taken place and proceeded to enter my home. My first stop was the mirror in the foyer bathroom. Sure enough, my left eye was totally swollen shut. I was also in a mild state of shock. I sat down on the stairs and gathered my thoughts. After a few moments, I began to pray. "Dear Lord, I do not know what to do and I am very concerned about my eye. Please lead me as to what to do." After praying, I felt led to wash my face with cold water. I did so and looked in the mirror. My eye was totally healed! To say the least, I was thrilled.

I set out to retrieve my lawn mower, hoping the wasps had settled down and moved on. En route to the mower, I saw the same neighbor I had spoken with only 3 – 4 minutes earlier. Again she paused from her chores and was amazed at the condition of my eye. "What did you take to heal it so quickly?" she asked. "Since you asked, I'll tell you," I replied, and did so. Her response was "no, really, what medicine did you take?" I restated the 4 minutes of my life that took place between our conversations. As she shook her head in disbelief, I departed and retrieved my lawn mower without further incident.

Growing in My Faith

March 15, 1984, was the day I became a permanent member of the family of God. When I returned to my office, following my prayer on Route 202, I called my friend Steve to share with him concerning the decision I had made. He was ecstatic! I remember asking him, "What do I do now?" His response was classic God: "Read your Bible every day, pray in the name of Jesus, and God will do the rest." He added, "you should also join a Bible-teaching church as the Lord leads you." However, he was unable even to recommend one because he lived 40 miles from Langhorne, PA and was not familiar with the local churches.

As I carried out his instructions, I also set aside 2-3 hours to walk in the woods on Sunday morning. What a time of blessing! Each Sunday morning it was just me and God (plus my 90-pound coonhound-mix, Behn), one on one. I remembered well the words of my friend and now brother, Boyd. "Tell God all you are thinking and feeling. Be real and leave out nothing." His love for me covers all parts of my life. God used it all — my one-on-one walks, daily Bible-reading and prayer time.

My first church experience was less than I had hoped for. After about 7 months with that congregation, I again called my friend Steve to express my frustration. He encouraged me to go with that which gave me peace and to trust in God. So, for about 9 months I stayed the course in the park, in God's Word daily, and in prayer.

Then late one Monday night, as I was watching Monday Night Football, there came a knock at my door. Holding back my dog (which saw these two men as a snack!), I met Mitch and Bill. They introduced themselves as Christian believers and wanted to invite me to a local Bible study! That seemed good to me. I remember asking them where they got may name and address. They could not remember! They knew they had my name and had to stop, even though it was very late at night. I told them I would pray about attending the study and they said goodnight. I remember thinking to myself, "Now there go two whacked-out guys." However, as I have learned, God frequently colors outside the lines of what we consider normal. I did pray, and was led by the Spirit to attend the study. I was blessed there in many ways. Life-long friendships were developed, and I was introduced to some good local Bible churches. I sat under great teaching and the door was opened for me to begin to serve others.

This season of waiting, in combination with the study, were significant stepping stones on my spiritual path. Yes, God is good, all the time. All things happen for the good for those who love Him and are called according to His purpose (Romans 8:28).

Obedience is Better than Sacrifice

As I became involved at a local church body, growth was beginning in many areas of my life. About one year into my time with this body of believers, God was blessing me with some special people. One of the more special was a man named Don. Don was a one-man greeting team. All the kids loved him. It seemed as if his pockets held an infinite supply of gum and candy for the children. One day, Don and his wife Hazel reached out to me and invited me to brunch after church. I accepted, and had a wonderful time of sharing and love. The food was pretty good, too. I thanked them and the Lord for blessing us as he had.

The next day, while I was in prayer, I felt led to call Don. I did not know why, and really had nothing to say to him that hadn't been said yesterday. I did not make the call. The next day, the same thought came to me. This was no longer a coincidence, of that I was sure. I intended to call Don, even just to say hello and "I love you." I did not make the call. I guess I got too busy and just forgot. It happened for the third time, and I was 100% sure I needed to make that phone call.

However, I didn't place the call. The next day, Don died. I was crushed. God gave me the opportunity to share in loving Don one more time and I didn't take advantage of it.

I promised myself that day: Never again. I would much rather appear foolish or uninformed than be disobedient. When I get to heaven, telling Don I love him is going to be high on my list of things to do.

An Ad in the Yellow Pages

In the summer of 1986, my printing company had a near-fatal experience. We had allowed an insurance company to become 60% of our business due to their rapid growth. We had a written contract and years worth of a great relationship. However, greed set into the heart of the insurance company's CEO. The contract allowed for termination, in writing, for any one of three reasons. I was told verbally that the contract was being terminated for none of those three reasons. It was because "we feel we can do better."

Panic set into the hearts of many of my employees and suppliers alike. We did all we could from a sales perspective and with internal belt-tightening. About three months after the announcement, we received a letter in the mail from a very large medical publisher. The letter notified us that they were closing their huge printing plant and were looking for vendors to fill certain niches of their printing needs. If we were interested in pursuing this, we were to fill out a preliminary information sheet and send it back. About a month later, we were called and told that in our area of expertise (advertising brochures), the customer was requesting a plant tour. The group came in about a week later and spent a few hours. They checked procedures and equipment, spoke to department heads, and reviewed the company from top to bottom. As we settled into the conference room for a time of review, they shared the scope of the commitment and where we stood. Although this was unofficial, we were told that we stood at the head of the class of the 12 companies that were being toured. Can you spell HAPPY?

They went on to discuss the steps of implementation in terms of schedule and volume. When it seemed as though all of the bases had been covered, we were asked if there were any questions remaining. "Yes, I said, "just one. When we received the original letter of inquiry, how or where did you get our name?" At this point, the vice president turned to his assistant and said, "She handled all of that for me at that stage." She then confidently added: "I saw your ad in the Yellow Pages. That is where I got all the names." I smiled and thought to myself, "Thank you, Jesus." At that, I expressed my gratitude for the opportunity and restated our commitment to the quality and service they would require. "However," I said, "There is one thing you need to know. We do not have an ad in any Yellow Pages, and never have had one." They were shocked. "Are you sure?" the assistant asked incredulously. At that moment, I thanked God for them. The Vice President agreed with me, while his assistant was still shaking her head.

The relationship forged that day was maintained to the day my company was merged out of existence in 1999. That firm was one of our best customers for 13 years. To God be the glory!

God Shows Himself to a Believer – ME!

In the fall of 1988, I received an invitation to attend an evening service at a church in North Central New Jersey. Since the invitation came from an attractive young woman, I did what any single guy would do. I said yes!

As it turned out, this body of believers was much more charismatic in nature than I was accustomed to. The service was alive, and the message was good. Before the service closed, the pastor called the assistant pastors and elders up to the pulpit. They were going to lay hands and pray for healing on two people who were scheduled for major surgery in the coming week. One man was in a wheel chair, and a woman needed assistance to make it forward.

Just before they began to pray, the pastor asked the 1,500 congregants to please pray in faith for the two people. Also, he suggested that anyone there that night who had anything wrong with them should place their hand on the part of their body that was hurting, and they also would be healed. Well, I found this to be amusing, and I actually laughed out loud. Needless to say, I was the only one laughing. As the prayer began, I gathered myself together and actually realized that my left shoulder was in pain. This was an old ice hockey injury. With much doubt in my heart, I thought "I have nothing to lose!" I placed my right hand on my left shoulder. When the prayer was over, my pain was gone! It has been almost 20 years, and my shoulder has never hurt once since that night.

Praise God, my heart was healed of doubt and God used my shoulder to get the job done. Yes, Lord, You are Jehovah Rapha.

Airport Delays

Early in my walk of faith, I discovered that my cousins in Texas had also become fulfilled Jews and our relationship immediately became much closer. In 1989 I set out to visit my family there. I had flown to Dallas a few times before on a direct, non-stop basis. This time, however, I could not book a non-stop flight. The only flight available went through Chicago, very early in the morning. So I bit the bullet and set out on my journey.

Upon arriving at O'Hare International Airport, I settled in at the waiting area to await my connecting flight. A few minutes later, a disheveled, smelly drunk came by. He looked at me and asked if the seat next to me was open. "Yes," I replied, but my thoughts were much less welcoming. "Do I really need to deal with someone like this at 7:00 a.m.?" I wondered. I remember telling God that I was not about to engage this man in conversation.

The man started asking me questions almost immediately! At first, the questions were basic: we discussed hangovers and remedies, a subject with which I had ample experience. The Holy Spirit reminded me that just a few years ago, I was in the same position as this man. His next topic was curiosity about where I was from. Upon learning that I was from Pennsylvania, he asked "Isn't that where the Amish and Mennonites are?" Then the conversation began to flow toward God. I knew right away that this was a Divine Appointment.

First, one week prior to this meeting I had watched a video on the history of the Amish and Mennonite churches. I was well-prepped for this subject! Second, the airline announced a one-hour flight delay... well, this man was duly impressed by my knowledge of this subject. As we explored the things of God, the moment was taking shape. After some time, he opened up and said that he had been raised in a church-going, Bible-believing family. However, his eyes had witnessed hypocrisy that sadly disappointed him. At this point, I excused myself for a trip to the men's room and a moment of quiet prayer. (Yes, you are allowed to pray in the bathroom!)

Upon returning, I up-tempoed the conversation, guiding him toward making an about-face in life and moving toward God. His response was "it's obvious that you have been raised in a good Christian family. However, I am too far gone. The bridge I would need to cross is too wide." My whole life was the answer to his statement, and I shared it. "Gordon, that's not true. You see, I am Jewish. In addition, just a few years ago I was heavily into drugs, alcohol, gambling and excessive partying. If Jesus can save me and turn my life around, does He love you any less?" He excused himself for a trip to the men's room.

We continued our conversation when he returned. We were given a 5 minute boarding notice by the flight attendant, but I reached out one more time. "Look, after we get on this plane, I may never see you again. Who knows what life has for us an hour from now," I said. "Put your stake in the soil today, right now. Let this be the moment you stood for Jesus Christ." "You mean, right here?" he asked. "Yes, right here," I replied.

With well over 100 people nearby as witnesses, he said a simple prayer and was born anew. We exchanged hugs, names and telephone numbers as we were boarding the aircraft. It turns out that this man is a very successful orthopedic surgeon. He was returning from a five-day, continuing education seminar. For him and a few friends, it was an annual drinking binge.

We all have bridges to cross in life. If you want to go it alone or just stay where you are, that's your choice. However, if you want to take a step toward God, He will always draw near to you as you draw near to Him.

God is at Work, Even When I Can't See It

About two and a half years into my walk with God, I was attending a sound Bible-teaching church that emphasized home fellowships. This small body within the larger body of believers is an ideal venue for personal growth, care and service. It is no coincidence that this is the exact format God chose to grow His family of believers for the first 300 years.

There I sat, in a home filled with love, with a dozen or more believers who all loved me. We sang praises together, shared from our hearts, studied scripture, prayed for each other, laughed and sometimes cried together. For the first six months or so, I said very little. When I did speak, my comments and questions often brought laughter (in love). One night I asked everyone to pray that God would bring me a good Christian wife. Everyone joyfully responded to my request. It would be helpful for you to understand my thinking. My old life-style was unacceptable before God. Celibacy was not an option. That left marriage.

Unbeknownst to me, as these prayers were being lifted up to God, He was busy working in the heart of Deborah Davis, my future wife. Deborah was living 3,000 miles away in San Francisco. Her life was less than she wanted, largely due to the fact that she was calling the shots rather than letting God rule her life. She made the decision that it was time too move back home to Newtown, PA to assist her ailing parents and have a fresh, recommitted start with God.

Perhaps six months later, Deborah and I crossed paths at a networking function of the Business Marketing Association. Deborah was there with her sister, Diane, who had once been my customer. I waved to Diane and walked over to say hello. As the dinner/speaker portion of the evening came, we sat together. In classic God fashion, the five people on our side of the table for 10 were all committed Christians, unknown to each of us before that dinner. One of the things Deborah shared was her search for a church home. I invited her to the church I attended, and she accepted.

For about four years, we interacted but never dated. We interacted at church. We played in a co-ed volleyball league together, and bicycled together with a group of 20-plus friends. We went on group trips with other Christian singles. Deborah is a writer and I am in the printing business, so we also interacted as both customer and supplier to each other. She purchased printing from me, and I purchased writing services from her on creative projects.

We knew each other as well as non-married people could, or so we thought. One day in May, 1990, I was brushing my teeth in the morning. Somehow the Holy Spirit spoke to me at that moment, and I knew that Deborah – my best friend – was to be my wife. During the next few weeks, we actually started acting as if we were dating. It all began when I reached over at a red light and kissed her in a way I had never kissed her before. I had already met her dad, Chassie, and her mom, Phyllis. They were the best. On or about week three of our dating, I decided it was time to get engaged.

Let's roll back the clock four years. After those prayers were lifted up at the home fellowship, I felt led of God to go and get ready. I took some loose diamonds I had purchased from a drug dealer — some years prior to my commitment to Christ! — out of my safe deposit box and went to see my jeweler. I explained that I wanted to have an engagement ring made with the largest stone, and a wedding band made from the smaller stones. "Great idea," he said. "Bring your fiancé in and we'll fit her for size." "Well, you see, I'm not dating anyone at the moment," I replied. "God told me to go and get ready, so why don't you just use your best judgment regarding the size?" He laughed and told me to come back in a week to pick up the rings. I did that, and back to the safe deposit box went the jewelry.

Fast forward again, and here were Deborah and I on date number three. As we set out, I proposed marriage to her in the car. She accepted, took the ring, placed it on her finger – and it was a perfect fit! No adjustments were required. She was surprised at the fit, so I shared the story with her. Eight weeks later we were married. By the way, the rest of the wedding plans followed the same story line: We prayed, and God answered.

For instance, the country club reception room was available after the agent had laughed at our short-notice request.

Deborah's wedding gown, which the store sales staff said would take up to 3 months to make, was selected off the rack with no alterations required. Even the wedding invitations, which were ordered at 5:00 p.m. on a Tuesday, arrived at Noon on Friday of the same week! No rush charges were paid for the printing and the freight was UPS ground transportation.

At the ripe young age of 44, I was married. More important, I am married to a beautiful woman and the great mother of our two children. I must confess that during that four-plus year wait, my faith faltered many times. I complained to God often. However, His love for me and for Deborah provided the perfect union at the perfect time. That is just the kind of friend He is. Thank you, Jesus, for being just who You are.

Name That Child

During our brief engagement, Deborah and I would discuss the topic of children. We were in agreement that we wanted children. While we were on our honeymoon, the subject came up again. It seemed like the number two was where we were having our peace, one boy and one girl. Proceeding along this avenue, we asked each other for names to fit this scenario. The names "Sara" and "Jesse" were our choices. No one else was aware of these conversations.

After our honeymoon, Deborah left on a three-week business trip to the west coast. I rendezvoused with her at the tail end of the trip and met many of her west coast friends from the 20 years she lived there. One friend threw a party in our honor. Another friend provided us with lodging. The day we were leaving, we were gathered in the living room in the early morning for coffee. Our hosts had a five-year-old little girl who was playing with her dolls. I asked her for the name of the doll she was playing with, and she replied "This doll has no name." She then ran out of the room and returned with a new doll. I repeated my question – "What's that doll's name?" She answered, "Sara."

Again she ran out of the room and returned with a new doll. I repeated my question for the third time – "What's that doll's name?" She said "Jesse."

Deborah and I looked at each other in amazement, saying nothing to each other. The child's mother interjected, "Who do you know named Sara and Jesse?" Her reply was classic: "Oh, no one!"

Through the mouth of this little child, God confirmed for us that He intended to give us the desire of our hearts. Thank you, Lord.

God Can (And Will!) Use Everyone, Just Where They Are

I am a businessman, so it makes sense that God would use me in the world of business. One day, one of my employees came into my office to see me, asking for a few moments of my time. When I assured him of his welcome, he closed the door and sat down. The closed door clued me in that this was not to be a light conversation.

Bill shared his heart with me, telling me he had cancer and it was really bad. He was being treated at one of the best facilities in the area, Fox Chase Cancer Center, and they held out almost no hope for him. He also shared that he had listened to the many things I'd said about Jesus over the last few years, but had been careful to keep the subject out of his heart. Now that he was dying, he wanted to embrace Jesus by faith. However, he felt guilty because he was only taking this step because he was dying.

You can imagine my shock and dismay. I closed my eyes for a moment to offer up a quick prayer for help, some words I could offer Bill from Jesus. "Suppose I told you I'd just gotten a phone call from God, and He told me you were going to be healed," I said. "Would you want to invite Jesus into your heart as Lord?" "Yes," he replied. "Suppose I told you I'd just gotten a phone call from God and He told me you were going to die," I continued. "Would you still want Jesus to be your Lord?" Again he said yes. "Well, if the answer is yes either way, where do you think the guilt is coming from?" I asked. "It's obvious," Bill said. "From Satan." He and I prayed together, and at that moment, Bill's eternal security was sealed.

Shortly thereafter, he headed off to Fox Chase Cancer Center for extended in-patient care. Bill remained heavy on my heart and I prayed regularly for him. A few days had passed and I was awakened from a sound sleep at about 4:00 a.m. So, I began to pray. I couldn't get back to sleep, so I prayed some more. Again, I was unable to get back to sleep. I surmised God was doing something more, here, and wanted my full attention. I got out of bed and onto my knees. After some time had passed, I heard a still, small voice in my heart that directed me to "Go to Fox Chase and pray with Bill. He will be healed." My response was to ask "Who are you talking to?" I stayed in prayer until I was sure that this message was for me. Then I arose, ate breakfast and sought the scriptures regarding healing. When the hour was reasonable, I called a few Christian brothers for accountability and counsel.

I set off to the hospital at around 10:00 a.m. Upon arrival, I quickly learned that if you are carrying a Bible, hospital staff members are very accommodating. I entered Bill's room to find him in very good spirits and glad to see me. We shared small talk for about a half hour. Just as I felt led to describe my early morning moments with Bill, his brother-in-law and a friend arrived. The small talk, now shared four ways, continued for another half hour. I became aware that Bill's brother-in-law planned to stay for at least three more hours, so I proceeded with that which the Lord had placed on my heart.

I began with prayer, and much to my surprise, all four of us participated. I told Bill about my early morning prayer time. He then shared with me that at that same hour, he'd awakened from a deep sleep and felt as if a wave of peace was enveloping him! He did not understand it, but loved every moment of the experience. With the three of us visitors gathered in prayer over Bill, in the name of Jesus we claimed the promises of Scripture, anointed him with oil, and left him in the loving arms of Christ.

As I was preparing to leave, one of Bill's doctors dropped in to check on him. He told Bill that the chemo portion of his treatment would start that day. "Excuse me, doctor, but my chemo was started three days ago," he replied. The physician was amazed that he had incorrect information, then asked Bill about the side effects he was experiencing. Bill said simply, "I have none." That alone was a major miracle, as chemo has more unpleasant side effects than one person could bear if he experienced them all.

As I left the hospital, I wasn't sure if my feet were actually touching the ground. I was blown away by what my Lord was doing and that He would allow me to be a small part of it. About three months later, Bill – the man with multiple cancer sites in his body, the man doctors gave no chance to live – returned to work, cancer-free.

A few months following Bill's return to work, he came to my office and again asked for a few minutes of my time. Again, he closed the door. "My heart is so filled with praise for God," he said. "However, I feel guilty because I am unable to share my new faith. I feel unworthy. I do not know the Bible well, I am basically shy," etc. My response was immediate and emphatic: "Forget the guilt! We both know its source. Second, praise God that you are unable to share your faith. Next time you're in prayer, tell God honestly of your feelings and your inability." He rarely wants your ability. He always wants your availability. Agreeing that was a fair course of action, he left.

Two weeks later, Bill appeared at my office door yet again. He asked for a few minutes of my time and yes, he closed the door. He told me that he had done what I had suggested. About a week after that, he went fishing upstate with an old friend, who had picked the fishing spot. They parked the car and walked for about an hour, found their spot and cast their lines into the water. His friend then turned to him and said, "So Bill, what's all this stuff I hear about you and Jesus?" For nearly five hours, Bill told me, all they did was fish and talk about the Lord. "I really didn't have to do anything," he said.

Yes, God wants to use you (and me), right where you are, with all of your inabilities. By the way, if you have any *abilities,* they are gifts from God, too!

Just Let Go of the Railing

A few years into my walk with God, my mother, Ida, shared with me that my faith in Jesus was "the best decision you ever made." I was excited to hear these words from my Jewish mom! As I wondered aloud why she would say this, she explained that the changes she'd seen in my life were so obviously for the better that she couldn't help but comment encouragingly.

I used this opportunity to once again share the pillars of my faith with her. However, she was still hung up on the many atrocities committed against Jews over the years, by people who called themselves Christian. I explained the difference between Christian and Gentile to no avail. She was also hung up on what others – my dad, her sister, other family members and friends – would say.

Some months later I received a telephone call from my dad that Mom had suffered a massive heart attack and was in intensive care. My two brothers and I visited our parents in Florida on a rotating basis. It was my turn to go, so off I went. Upon arriving at the hospital, it was clear Mom was near death. During the next 24 hours, three different doctors and the nurses on each of three shifts pulled me aside and told me that my mom was going to die. I proceeded to call my brothers and communicate this information. The message was simple: If you want to see Mom alive again, get on the next plane to Miami.

My dad was tired and decided to take a nap in the hospital's family waiting area. I used this opportunity to take a walk on the beach and talk to Jesus. As I was walking with Him an entire story flashed into my brain. It was the story of how I had learned to walk as a baby. I had no prior recollection of this story, nor any photos of the house in which the story took place. We moved out of this house when I was two-and-a-half years old. The Lord directed me to share this story with my mother, and added some additional commentary for her. All I could do was shake my head in amazement. There were 50 or more ways the story could be inaccurate! How could I know this story was correct?

As soon as I said "Yes, Lord, I'll go," a ball rolled into my path. I saw two children chasing it, picked it up before it entered the ocean, and rolled it back to the kids. Their dad approached me. "It was very nice of you to do that," he said. "Would you happen to be hungry? We are about to eat and would love for you to join us." Actually, I hadn't eaten for awhile and was happy to join them. We shared light, pleasant conversation along with the meal, and then I returned to the hospital.

With my dad still sleeping, I entered my mother's room, happy for the time to spend alone with her. Although she was very sick, she had a clear grip on her faculties and speech. I asked if I could tell her a story, and she said yes.

"This is the story of how I learned to walk as a baby," I began. "You and I were alone in our home on McKinley Street." (That was a strange statement, since my brothers were only four and seven years old at the time. My grandmother lived with us, and she spoke no English. My grandmother hated my father. We did not own a car. Where was everyone?) "It was just you and me," I continued. "You placed me at the base of the stairs from the bedroom level to the living room. The stairs were made of a medium brown-colored wood and covered with strip gray carpet. The railing was the same color and the newel posts were painted white. In the living room were a light blue sofa with brown wooden, carved feet; two ivory colored matching chairs; two leather-topped end tables with gold-laced and ivory decoration, a matching coffee table, and a gray area rug.

"I stood at the base of those stairs, holding on to the railing. You were on your knees in the center of the room, calling to me. I would not let go of the railing because I was scared," I told her. "You persisted in calling to me. Eventually, because I knew you loved me and wouldn't do something to hurt me, I overcame my fear, let go, and walked to you. That is how I learned to walk!"

She was amazed. "Every word you said is accurate!" she exclaimed. Who told you this story?" I shared my beach experience with her, and she was in awe, remarking again on how the story was 100% accurate. Then I proceeded with the personal message to her from God. "Mom, now the roles are reversed," I said. You are the one holding on to the railing, and Jesus is the one extending His arms of love to you. You need to let go of the things of the past and pay no regard to what others may say. Just trust in the fact that Jesus loves you and He is Lord of all." She did just that.

Early the next morning I brought my brother, Bob, to the hospital from the airport. When we entered the room, Ida, who had not eaten anything for a week, looked us both in the eye and asked "What do you have to do to get a decent meal in this place?"

She was healed, too! Two days later she was back home at my parents' apartment, where she remained for six months. When she went back to the hospital for a six month review and check-up, she suffered another heart attack. She is home today in heaven, and I praise God for that.

I Just Don't Know

My relationship with my father, Solomon, was never very good. He was a hard-working man and a good provider of the basics of life. We had a warm home, plenty of food, clothing, a good education, basic sports equipment and a few toys.

He was a very stubborn man, lacking in social graces or personal relationship skills. He maintained one view on life: "My way or the highway." As he got older, he developed a physical condition and habit that had always been a part of his real personality: He required hearing aids. If you initiated a deeply personal conversation, or ventured into a subject he didn't want to talk about, he simply took out his hearing aid and placed it on the table! This gesture illustrates the ultimate in being "tuned out."

When it came to spiritual matters, he was not at all interested. He knew that the major organized religions were riddled with fraud and that was all he needed to know. To him, God was whatever he wanted God to be. He refused to deal with his own sin issues or forgiveness of the sins of others. He was just a hard man.

I tried on many occasions to share the gospel of God's love

with him, but he simply didn't want to hear it. He would not hear of his wife's faith late in life. After Mom's death, it seemed he just decided he didn't want to live anymore and set out to die the best way he could. He stopped taking his medications, stopped eating or bathing properly, stopped exercising or anything else that would facilitate healthy living. His focus was on dying.

About a year after my mother's passing, he lay in a hospital bed near death. My brother Harold and I had been with him for three or four days, but since there was nothing truly physically wrong with him, we had no idea how long he would hang in there. So both of us said our good-byes and prepared to depart. Just as we were leaving for the airport, my father turned to me and said, in a very serious tone of voice, "Do you really believe all those things you have been telling me about God?" "Yes, Dad, I do," I replied. "From the bottom of my heart, it's all true." He then turned to Harold, who's an atheist, and asked "Do you believe in God?" Much to my shock, Harold said yes! As we left, I know my dad was seriously entertaining the truth of God.

A few days later, we were back in Florida for his funeral. Is my father in heaven? I just don't know. When I remind my brother of that bedside conversation, his response is always the same: "I do not remember any of that ever happening." Nevertheless, my memory is crystal clear. My dad was clearly examining his eternal choices. I just don't know what decision my father ultimately chose to make.

Accountability

It has been my experience that the words "change" (of self) and "accountability" are perhaps the two scariest words in the English language. Why is that? I think these two words lie at the crossroads of our fleshly person and the Kingdom-focused person God wants us to be. They are battle-line words. This is where the trench warfare of our hearts takes place: I have seen this in my own life, in the lives of those close to me, in the lives of pastors of churches large and small, in the lives of those financially well-off and of the poor. This is an area where we all struggle more than need be.

Instead of being fearful of these two words, we should embrace them as a blessing from God, a blessing more valuable than fine gold. About a year after we were married, Deborah and I set out to Mars, Pennsylvania, to a Fellowship of Companies for Christ International (FCCI) conference. FCCI comes along side of business people in a counseling capacity to encourage and equip them to apply the Word of God to their businesses. In fact, FCCI encouraged business owners and CEOs to see their position in life as their mission field. What a beautiful true picture.

At this conference, we began building relationships with people we still hold dear to our hearts today. The teaching was flat-out the best as well as voluminous. One of the last things we were presented with was this challenge: "Although you may have 20 pages of outlines and notes, pick not less than one and not more than two things you have learned here, and implement them immediately."

During the seven-hour ride home, Deborah and I were given a great time to share with each other as a follow-up to the conference. We were in agreement that applying accountability was at the top of our list with regard to our business. We had been given guidelines we could use immediately and that still guide our steps today.

1. Consult the Word of God on every decision.
2. Cover each decision with Prayer (individually and together). God intends married partners to operate in "oneness." Without the agreement of both parties, do nothing.
3. Have a prayer partner, a carefully chosen person. Ask the Holy Spirit for help in selecting the right person for you.
4. Assemble a Council of Advisors. A group of godly persons to whom we would hold ourselves accountable for decisions on ALL elements of the business/ministry.

While we were in oneness on inserting more accountability in our business (and personal) lives, we were left with the selection process. Who could we ask to be our counsel? After all, we were asking for a considerable commitment from these folks. We took 15 minutes to be still and seek the Lord for those names. After this time with God, we shared with each other.

First, we were in immediate agreement as to the number of people we should have on the council and on its format. We would be a council of seven, including me, Deborah and five others. Deborah and I would not get a vote on any decision. All decisions had to be unanimous, and even votes of four to one would constitute a red light, a signal not to proceed. Next came the actual names of the people we would ask to assist us. Of all the people we know, God gave each of us the same names as we sought him in our prayer closets! We were blown away by the oneness and peace we were experiencing. Probabilities like that only result via the hand of God. Praise the Lord.

We contacted each person and explained the concept and the counsel we hoped to receive from them. Each one prayed and agreed to serve. Since 1991, the faces of those on the council have periodically changed, yet it remains a source of incredible blessing. It is a tool God has used, and continues to use, to help us keep a Kingdom focus in spite of our natural tendencies.

God is so good.

Even the Rocks Will Cry Out

One Sunday shortly after we were married, Deborah had volunteered for nursery duty and, consequently, I sat by myself during the Sunday church service. This particular congregation's service had a free flow to its worship and format, and whenever the pastor felt a leading of the Holy Spirit, he would do his best to follow that leading. All was biblical, and praise God, the worship was a beautiful thing. This particular Sunday was such a day. Flowing out of the worship time, people stood up to praise God, ask for prayer, quote scripture, sing additional songs, etc. People stood, sat, knelt, raised their hands, or not – as each one was led.

As I was standing there, the Holy Spirit was prompting me to sing a song. To fully appreciate the irony, you need to understand that my voice has two keys – on and off! So, I did what any tone-deaf and tuneless person would do; I said "No."

A few minutes passed, and again, I felt the same leading. Again, I said "No." A few more minutes went by, and again, the same leading and the same answer. I still said "No." As a matter of fact, I recommended to God that He ask the fellow standing behind me to sing for Him, because that man had a wonderful voice! Still a few more minutes passed with me feeling this persistent leading, and finally I couldn't take it any more.

I began to belt out the song as best I could, hoping the congregation would join in and drown me out. No one uttered a word! At the very end of the song, the congregation finally joined me, and we corporately sang the chorus through again.

After church, most of the congregation gathered in the Fellowship Hall for coffee and pastries. A number of people were asking, "Who sang that beautiful song?" When I said it was me, they all laughed and countered "No, really, who sang that song?" I persisted, and shared the whole story, including my three refusals to God. Then the worship leader came up to me and said "I nearly wet myself when you started singing."

"Why," I asked, "was it that bad?" "Oh, no!" she replied, "You actually were quite good. It was hard to believe it was you singing (she had heard me sing before) except that I watched you do it. However, you don't understand," she said.

"God told me three times to sing 'I Am the God that Healeth Thee,' and three times I refused him. So when you started singing that particular song and did it so well, I could only think that if I, to whom He's given talent, won't do what God asks, then He will get the job done through someone with no talent at all!" He is rarely looking for my ability and almost always looking for my availability.

Love Them, Pray for Them, and Be Ready When God Opens the Door

When it came to marriage, I had no clue what to expect. My parents did not provide a godly role model and my life experiences were all about me and my selfish desires. I truly entered marriage as a faith decision. Correspondingly, I had no idea what I should expect in terms of a mother-in-law and father-in-law. Here again, God went before me and gave me two of the best people I could ever have hope for as my in-laws. Their names are Chassie and Phyllis Davis.

Shortly after getting to know them well, I discovered that Phyllis was a woman of Christian faith, but Chassie was not a man of Christian faith. He was talented, a good guy, a fun guy, a great dad and a wonderful father-in-law. But on God's agenda, all these good qualities fall short of His glory. Only through faith in Jesus as Savior and Lord of your life can one be a part of God's eternal family.

A few years into our marriage, Chassie found himself home alone for two weeks while Phyllis and two of her daughters were traveling in Europe. We had sent Chassie some "care packages" of food. In addition, we had him over to the house for dinner one night. I had been praying for an opportunity to talk to Chassie, one on one, for quite some time. After dinner, Deborah was giving our toddler daughter Sara a bath and preparing her for bedtime, and there were Chassie and I alone together on clean-up detail. The timing seemed perfect.

I asked him for permission to ask a few questions that were on my heart. He agreed that I could, and so I began. During the course of the conversation, I shared the Gospel truth of God's love and how it applied to Chassie. Although I tried to promote dialog, none was forthcoming. As a matter of fact, he did not return to our house for a year after than conversation. He is not alone in this kind of posturing.

However, this changed nothing. My call was to love my in-laws, not as a yes-man or a candy-man, but as a sensitive, caring man who doesn't lose sight of what real love is. I am also called to remain in prayer and ready when God opens the door.

Some years later, Chassie was diagnosed with bladder cancer. His initial surgery seemed successful, but that was not the case. About six months later, it was discovered his cancer had spread and his last days were drawing near. I visited him in Doylestown Hospital a few times. Chassie was a large man, very strong and very proud. By every standard there is in a man's realm, he was a "good guy." I went to see him one morning, only to find that he was unable to speak due to a throat that was very sore from using a breathing tube. So we chatted, using the "raise your hand" method for yes and no. Again I asked Chassie if I could pray for him. That morning I told him I would change my prayer, and that if he agreed with me after I had finished, just to raise his hand. I knew he understood the tenets of faith, so I began to pray. I thanked God for His love, for His provision in the person of Jesus Christ as Savior, for His biblical promises of heaven for all those who accept the free gift of forgiveness of all sins (past, present and future), and who desire of Jesus that He would be their Lord.

I had my eyes closed while praying. Before I opened them, I asked Chassie to raise his hand if he'd said that prayer in his heart and truly believed. When I opened my eyes, not only was his hand all the way up in the air, but streams of tears were running down his face! I had to get a tissue to clean him up a little. What a blessing – Praise God. An additional confirmation occurred later that day, when Phyllis arrived for her daily visit.

By that time, Chassie's voice had returned. Here lay a man who had essentially been mum with regard to God for his entire adult life. As Phyllis entered the room, he spoke out: "Phyllis, let's pray."

There are many people I can't wait to see again. Chassie, you are one of them.

Tithes, Gifts and Sacrifice

It is my belief that as you study the Scripture, the principle of tithing teaches that 10% of your first fruits belong to God. Gifts to God are anything more than that 10%. Sacrifice, to me, is when I give up something I really need to meet the needs of someone else with needs greater than mine. Some people will argue that this is an Old Testament point of view, and I would agree. However, the New Testament view is that it *all* belongs to God. After all, what do I have that He has not given me, with the hope that I would steward it with a total focus on God's Lordship? Enough said. You must decide in your own heart. God will supply the final answer to this question in His time.

We regularly apply this principle of tithing and gifts in our home. However, as a couple we have never been called to sacrifice. As a matter of fact, I personally know of only two families who actually have. Here is the one story in which I had a part.

I was an elder at the church where Deborah and I were married. One year, I was a member of the Needy Fund Committee. This committee consisted of the head elder plus three others. One month, we were gathering for our meeting to review the requests presented to us. Some of these requests involved money, counseling, goods, services or any combination thereof. After we had considered the written requests at hand, one of the other elders said he felt the Holy Spirit had put an elderly couple in the church on his heart. This was the first time a leading like this had ever occurred within the meetings. The process was simply that requests were presented in writing through the church office, and occasionally these requests came to us verbally. But we went to prayer for confirmation on the leading of this elder.

After a few minutes, we were all in oneness. We then went to prayer again, asking God how much we should give or what else we should do. Again we completely agreed after a few minutes in prayer. We understood that we were to disburse a sum of $500.00 to this elderly couple in the church family. This was a considerable amount, since we had only $1,200.00 in the fund itself. But we obeyed and immediately mailed a check to the couple.

The following Sunday, the elderly man came up to me, nearly in tears, to thank me for the money. I explained what had happened, and we both gave praise to God. But he wasn't finished. "There's a part of the story that you don't know about," he said. He proceeded to share with me that two weeks earlier, a missionary in desperate need of $50.00 had approached him and his wife with a request for assistance. He told the missionary that they were on a very tight, fixed budget with not a dollar extra to spare, but he and his wife would pray about it. After prayer, the couple believed the Lord was telling them to send the man the $50.00. The only way they could accommodate this was to fast for a week, using their food budget for the donation. They mailed out that $50.00.

That afternoon, as he retrieved and sorted through his mail, there was our check for $500.00! All this couple could do was cry from thanksgiving and joy. Praise God, He is so faithful to His Word and as my friend.

Late for Work

I owned and operated a printing plant from 1979 to 1998. For about 12 of those years, a young man named Mike worked for me in customer service and then in sales. Mike was an alcoholic, among his other vices. As a result, he would often be late for work. We had an employee handbook that outlined our policy with regard to tardiness.

Accordingly, Mike's actions had cost him loss of pay many times. He should have been terminated. However, every time I prayed for Mike, God said "No, you cannot fire him." Mike had been attending out Bible study at work, but his motive was earning brownie points, not seriously seeking knowledge of the Lord.

Some years into our working relationship, Mike was having lunch on a park bench in Washington Square, in center city Philadelphia. It was a beautiful, sunny day. Much to his surprise, as he sat there, the Holy Spirit descended upon him. Suddenly, the words he'd not really been listening to rang true. With tears rolling down his face and a heart filled with thanksgiving, he invited Jesus into his heart to be his Lord and Savior. Praise be to God.

Mike returned to the office later that afternoon to share his story with me. We hugged, prayed and gave thanks to Jesus together. However, over the next year plus, he was *still* regularly late for work. No longer was he hung over, just caught in a bad habit he could not break. Meanwhile, other non-believing employees were watching and sometimes commenting on Mike's conduct, referring to the employee handbook. Together, Mike and I tried a series of incentives, punitive measures, his plan, my plan, as well as regular prayer. Nothing worked. He even told me he deserved to be fired. But when I prayed about it, God again said "No." I was so frustrated that I simply gave it over into God's hands. "He's yours, and I give up! I am not even going to pray for him anymore!"

Mike heard and ignored a knock at his door a few weeks later. He lived in a row home in South Philadelphia, and it was close to midnight – not the time to be opening your door to who knows what situation. The wind was howling, and it was bitterly cold outside. Again, Mike heard the knock at his door. He cautiously went to the door and peeked out, but saw no one. As he opened the door wider to look around the street, a half frozen dog ran into his house. There was no one else there (that he could see). Feeling sorry for the dog, Mike's plan was to give the animal some food, water and a warm place to stay, just for the night. In the morning, he would attempt to find the dog's owner.

The next morning, the dog got him up early by licking his face. Guess what?

Mike was on time for work that day, and every day thereafter. This dog (now named Lucky), was a gift from God, who loves him.

Prayer Walk

Early one morning in the fall of 1994, I was up and out of the house while it was still dark, taking a prayer walk. Just me, Jesus and the quiet of the early morning – I love walking with God, sharing my heart and trying to be still enough to hear from Him. Although his methods and messages sometime seem strange to me, He has only my best interests at heart.

Deborah greeted me warmly when I returned home and asked, "What did God say to you this morning?" "I think He said it's time to sell our house in Cape May," I answered. "Sell our house in Cape May?" she gasped. "No way! God wouldn't say that!" We had owned this beautiful oceanfront home in New Jersey for eight years, and it had been a blessing to all who entered its doors. People were healed there. Singles fell in love and were later married. Couples conceived – Oops! The peace of the Lord was upon that place. We loved the house, the view, the town and everything related to it. And so we agreed, we would say nothing to anyone. Prayer was the only outlet we would pursue.

Perhaps a week after this conversation, we received a telephone call from a realtor friend of ours in Cape May. "You wouldn't by any chance be interested in selling your home, would you?" she asked. She had a client who specifically asked about the possible availability of our house! We merely said that we would get back to her. After more prayer, we felt the leading of the Lord and agreed to sell. We set a price, it was accepted, and we never met the folks until settlement. Settlement was in March of 1995. During the six months between the initial telephone call and settlement, our adoption plans hit full speed. Once again, God had prepared the way for our changing circumstances.

Do we miss the house? Sure we do. But the peace of obedience is far better.

God Will Make a Way – Again and Again

This is an animal-lover's story – as if previous stories were not! Deborah and I have always been "animal people," and each of us has given homes to an assortment of rescued dogs and cats over the years both before and after our marriage. When we were first married, we had one dog and four cats between us. We now have two dogs.

We had trimmed down the numbers in our cat herd to one, Joshua. He was a really terrific, fun and very good cat, loaded with personality. Unfortunately he had experienced just too much change in his life. Cats do not like change. He was with Deborah in San Francisco, where she rescued him through the SPCA. He lived with Deborah and her parents in Newtown, PA, when she moved back east, then lived with me when we got married, only to find three other cats and a 90-pound coon hound with which he had to share his home!

Joshua adjusted to each new phase of life as well as could be expected. However, when our daughter Sara came from China to live with us, the cat became very resentful. As a result, he would spray in her bedroom and on her toys. We tried giving Joshua extra attention. We tried medication, all to no avail. Someone suggested a change in diet, but that didn't work, either. Creative parenting, patience, and every other effort simply failed. By now, Sara was a toddler and we were expecting Jesse to join our family from Guatemala at any time. We prayed and prayed about what to do. We really loved Joshua, but we knew that a second child would only magnify the problem. With much pain in our hearts, we made the appointment to have Joshua put to sleep. He was a 12 year old healthy cat, and we were broken-hearted.

As I was driving, *en route* to the veterinarian's office, I called out to God through my tears. "Please, Lord," I prayed, "bring an elderly couple with no children across my path. They would be a perfect match for Joshua. If not that, then *something*, PLEASE!"

When I checked in at the vet's office, the kind technician took Joshua, in his carrier, to the rear of the facility. I remained in the waiting area for the return of the cat carrier. After about 15 minutes of waiting, I asked at the reception desk why it was taking so long to take a cat out of a carrier and place him in a cage. She understood my impatience and pain, and said "I'll check right away." Another 10 minutes went by, and then one of the veterinarians came out to see me. "Do you have a minute?" she asked. I answered "Sure," and followed her to the rear of the hospital.

She explained to me that the hospital maintained a small cattery of 10 to 12 animals as a blood bank. Each cat donates blood as needed, but never more often than once a month. These were all hard-to-place cats, although they did try to place them for adoption. As it worked out, they had just placed two of their cats into homes and had an opening for a new feline blood donor. Each cat had its own cubicle with an open door, in an enclosed room. There was plenty of food, medical attention if needed, other cats to play with, and a student who came in daily for grooming and fun. The vet asked if I would allow Joshua to live there.

My answer was an enthusiastic "YES!"

Deborah was ecstatic when she learned of this miracle. We never went to see Joshua, fearing that seeing us would make it more difficult for him to adjust to one more change. However, we did inquire of him periodically. He reportedly was happy, healthy and well adjusted for his last three years of life.

God is so good. As His family, He promised He would never leave us or forsake us. All I can say is "Thank you."

Hearing, but Not Listening

In the spring of 1995, I went on a retreat to South Carolina with four other men from our church. Retreats are always a blessing, whether I have one hour in the park or 5 days in South Carolina.

Early in the morning of the fourth day, I left the motel room to take a prayer walk. How beautiful it is just to be one-on-one with my best friend. I shared many issues that were in my heart with God, and I remember His ministering with love to me every step of the way. About 10 minutes before my walk ended, I asked God if there was anything He wanted me to do. I really expected an "atta-boy" or some similar accolade for an answer. I was wrong, again.

He placed on my heart the need to warn a member of the group I was traveling with. This man was very overweight and diabetic. His eating habits, especially with regard to sweets, were a real problem. I was not looking forward to carrying out this assignment, because this man wasn't usually open in nature. He relied heavily on his own understanding and desires to direct his paths.

Shortly after the sun came up I approached my compatriot,

seizing an opportunity when we could be alone. I asked his permission to share something personal with him. He agreed, and I proceeded to warn him as the Lord had directed me about controlling his eating habits for the sake of his health. The man was taken aback, and asked me quite a few questions that required my opinion for answers. I was careful in answering him and emphasized that these were my *opinions*. I prayed continuously during our conversation. After about 15 minutes, he guardedly and coolly thanked me, and then we departed for breakfast.

As we gathered in the main conference room for the first session of the morning, we found that the first speaker of the morning was an African American pastor from Dallas, TX. I had never heard of this man before, and, in fact, have never heard of him since that day.

His commentary took a detour only a few minutes into his message. He said so himself, as he just felt led to move into a topic other than the one he'd prepared. For the next 15 minutes, he proceeded to say everything I had said earlier that morning to my associate! He even used many of the sentences I spoke, word for word, including some slang expressions. Neither of us could believe what we were hearing. My associate had now clearly heard from God, twice.

Let's fast-forward two days. When he arrived home, he shared my comments with his wife. She agreed with every word and confirmed the entire experience. This was now three times he had heard from God that I know of, through three different messengers. However, he continued to walk in disobedience and during the next few years suffered greatly from his deteriorating medical condition. Another shot of insulin could no longer be the "fix it."

When it comes to spiritual matters, each of us must seek the Lord on our own. The best way to seek His guidance is through His written word, the Bible, and through the leading of the Holy Spirit. In combination, you will never go wrong. Sometimes, God will even use someone else for a minder or a confirmation. However, getting the message is only the smaller part of the deal. Obedience to the message is where the real battle takes place. We have a spiritual adversary who has only two goals: One is to keep us from God through belief in Jesus Christ, and the second is to minimize our walk with Jesus. In addition, we have the challenge of our own stubborn hearts. The problem here is that our hearts, by their own nature, want to deceive us with regard to godly issues. Our hearts are naturally wicked and selfish when it comes to things of God. The good news is that Jesus will overcome all of these issues when we avail our lives to His Lordship. The truth really does set you free.

Coloring Outside the Lines

Deborah and I sort of lived life backward compared with many couples. After college and the military (for me), we separately set out to establish our careers, party, and party some more. By the time God seriously got our attention, we were older. We were married August 11, 1990. By then, I was pushing 44 and Deborah was 39. Largely due to our ages, we had difficulty having children. Deborah had a few miscarriages, and we realized that adoption was the way to go. Finding an agency that would permit us to adopt an infant at our ripe old ages was harder than expected, but once again, God found a way. Through a tiny classified ad that came to Deborah's mother's attention, we found an organization that was helping couples adopt babies from China when it was a relatively new phenomenon.

Eleven months after we started the process, Sara Lin was our little girl. We had only a tiny picture and the Lord's leading to go on when we accepted her from the adoption arm of the People's Republic of China. She was a beautiful 14-month-old and extremely underdeveloped due to conditions in the orphanage in China. Deborah traveled to China without me but with a social worker and two other couples with whom we remain close friends. I stayed home because the call to go caught us between moving into our new house and selling the old one. We also had two businesses to look after as well as pets to be considered. After prayer, this seemed to us to be the best option.

From Day One, Sara has been a blessing with an incredibly sunny disposition. She grew rapidly as we nurtured and nourished her, despite bouts with upper respiratory infections, Ascaris worms and a few other issues. Sara went quickly from lying down, to standing, to walking fairly quickly, but she never crawled. As she developed she would fall a lot. The more she grew, the clearer it became that she was actually tripping herself more than could be considered normal, even with her shaky start in life. She also had an aversion to walking on grass or any surface that was not hard and flat, as she would lose her balance and fall almost immediately.

We consulted her pediatrician, who referred us on to Children's Hospital in Philadelphia. After her examinations there, we were given a diagnosis of cerebral palsy, fairly mild, for which there was no medication or surgery. We were told that the cause was probably an *in utero* stroke, so while the damage was done and would not get worse, we needed to watch for new symptoms to emerge and see what issues Sara would face as she grew physically and developed mentally.

To say that we were devastated would be an understatement. The more we observed Sara, the more we realized that this was affecting her entire right side. Her right leg was turned inward, and her right foot even more so. She was fitted for a brace to help her walk and keep her tendons stretched at night. Her right arm and hand were far less functional than her left side, even though she is a "right dominant" child. There was only one place left to go: to Dr. Jesus.

We were led through prayer to scripture in James, which in turn led us to the elders of the church we were attending. We were actually between church homes at the time, but had regularly been visiting a local, very conservative body for several months. We called the pastor and presented our request to have the elders pray over Sara and anoint her with oil for the purpose of being healed. Although familiar with the scripture, the pastor said that the elders probably would not agree to our request because of their very conservative posture on such issues. However, he also said ours was the second telephone call he'd received that day for the exact same purpose, so could he please get back to us? We agreed, and a few days later he did call back. His question to us was whether we would be amenable to a healing service. Neither he nor this church body had ever held such a service before, but this was the action he believed the Holy Spirit was leading him to take. We decided we would participate, and the date was set for a Friday night two weeks later.

We and many of our friends were offering fervent prayer covering over the coming evening. As I was in prayer a few days after my conversation with the pastor, I believe the Lord told me that I was to use my prayer *talis* as part of the service. After extensive searching, I was surprised to actually find it among my possessions. I had not touched it for 35 years except to pack it up and move it when changing residences. We called the pastor to seek and receive his OK. As he explained to us, "There's no formula here; we're all walking by faith."

Only a few days later, an old friend stopped by our house, a very sweet Italian lady named Kay. She shared with us that she, too, was deep in prayer regarding Sara's health issues. In the quiet of her prayer time, God had told her to go and get me a *talis*, which she purchased from a local synagogue. Wanting to know more about prayer shawls, she researched the *talis* from a Messianic perspective. She gave me four typewritten pages of information, nearly none of which had I seen before. It revealed some fascinating points.

First, the *talis* (which means small tent) came into being because it was impossible for 6,000,000 people to visit the Holy of Holies in the desert during the 40 years the Israelites wandered in the wilderness with Moses after leaving Egypt. Each male head of household was linked in oneness to God via the prayer shawl. Second, the shawl has 39 sets of tassels, the same number of stripes Jesus bore on our behalf. "By his stripes we are healed (Isaiah 53:5). Third, three incidents are recorded in the Bible (Matthew 9:20, 14:36 and Luke 8:44) where the touching of Jesus' prayer shawl (garment) resulted in healing. In addition, I was always taught that the apostle Paul was a tent maker. There is a great likelihood that he in fact was a *talis* maker. This possibility is in line with his religious training prior to being fulfilled.

I thanked Kay for her gift, especially for the research information. The truth really does set you free. Just a few days later, another dear friend called. Her name is Karen and she is of Swedish heritage. She shared with me that she and her husband Wes, of Dutch heritage, would attend the service and had been in prayer for Sara's healing. "By the way," she said, "you wouldn't happen to know where I could get a *talis*, would you? I know it seems weird, but God has placed on our hearts that we should have one for the service." I gave her the extra *talis*, a copy of the research, and the story of Kay's gift.

The night of the healing service finally came. Sara, who was now about three years old, Deborah and I arrived for our special appointment with God. After some scripture and guidelines were read from pulpit, the congregation was led in praise through music and song. As led by the Lord, each family seeking healing came forward. The pastor and two elders prayed over the sick person and anointed each with oil in the name of Jesus. When we felt the time was right, we also walked forward as a family. First, I took out the shawl, said the corresponding prayers that go with donning it, and draped it over the three of us. The pastor and elders did their part and gave us the nod to return to our seats. Sara ran in front of Deborah and me. She did not fall! Her leg, foot and entire right side were healed! We could only look tearfully into each others' eyes and praise the Lord.

That night, 12 of the 15 families who went forward during the service claimed a healing. I am unable to substantiate the claims of anyone else for healing during that special service. But as sure as the sun rises in the east and sets in the west, that's how sure I am of Sara's healing. Today she is very active in soccer, karate, swimming and sports in general. She still must use some different learning techniques than other students as her stroke did affect her brain's language center. But she is bright, strong and beautiful, and does very well in regular academic classes.

There are no words to express the gratitude in our hearts. "Thank you, Lord Jesus," is the best we can do.

God Continues to Bless Us

In April of 1997, Deborah and I received a joyous telephone call from our social worker at the adoption agency. We had a son waiting for us in Guatemala and he was three days old. Due to government regulations, Jesse lived with a foster family in Guatemala City from the time he was seven days old until he was four months old. At that point we could travel to Guatemala to bring him home. Unlike our China experience, we had four months' notice and could plan more effectively for this trip.

One thing that was not in our plans was the injury to my right knee that I sustained while playing softball. I had torn my meniscus approximately a month before the trip. Because the pain was manageable, I decided to put the surgery off until after we returned.

Much like with our first adoption where I stayed home, Deborah stayed home with Sara and kept the home fires burning. I traveled to Guatemala with a social worker and another adoptive mother. There were no real hitches on this trip, which was a blessing in itself. You see, Guatemala was in the middle of a civil war at the time and bad things were happening daily. After only three days, I returned home with our beautiful son. Deborah and Sara met us at the airport. As we exited the plane, we were greeted with hugs, kisses and praises. Within 15 to 20 yards of our walk toward the baggage claim, our sweet and joy-filled little Sara — who had been so excited about the arrival of her new baby brother – began to act out. The sibling rivalry had already begun!

I had my knee surgery within a few days of returning home. The evening after the operation, I was sitting on the floor of the living room, trying to do my prescribed exercises which were to be followed by ice wraps. Out of the bedroom came a scream!

Jesse, who hated diaper changes, had been flailing about on the changing table and nearly rolled off while Deborah's attention was turned to picking up the powder container he'd knocked away. To prevent him from falling to the floor, Deborah had grabbed for him and gotten his arm, which now lay limp as he lay screaming. Jesse was screaming, Deborah was very upset, I was out of action on the floor and Sara was three and half years old. We decided it was best to take him to the hospital emergency room. With Jesse strapped into his car seat, Deborah drove the five minutes it took to reach the hospital by car while Sara and I prayed at home.

Just as they got to the emergency room, Jesse stopped crying. They were met by a doctor and Deborah very quickly told him what had happened. The doctor examined Jesse and concluded that his elbow had been dislocated, but it had been re-set perfectly, and the doctor wanted to know who had worked on the little limb. It had to have been God. There was no one else in the back seat. Deborah and Jesse returned home a scant half-hour after they'd left. Praise God, He never leaves us or forsakes us.

Things Aren't Always What They Seem to Be

It was August, 1997, and I was *en route* to Guatemala to pick up our son, Jesse. The trip required a change of planes in Houston, Texas and I had about two hours between flights. Due to my state of anxiety and excitement, I thought the best thing for me to do was to take a long walk through the airport. One of the first shops I noticed was a fudge shop. I thought, "I'd better stop here last. Otherwise, I will stop in there twice!"

After my leisurely stroll, into the fudge shop I went. Greeting me was an attractive young woman with a very soft, pleasant manner. We engaged in some light conversation about life. As we spoke, I could not help but sense a strong feeling of peace. I was probably in that shop for 15 or 20 minutes, keeping an eye on the clock lest I miss my flight. I finalized my purchase and noticed her jewelry. This woman was wearing a gold cross on one lapel and a pair of gold doves on the other. As she handed me my package and change, I was overwhelmed with the need to give her a witnessing card explaining the tenets of Christian faith from the stash I generally keep in my wallet.

I remember thinking to myself, "This is silly. She is obviously a Christian." However, I followed the leading and gave her a "Thank You" card with a message about Christ's gift of salvation to us through His death and resurrection. I even went so far as to explain to her that it "might not be for you. Maybe it's for a friend of yours. I only know that I have to give it to you." She paused and read the card. "This is so wonderful," she exclaimed. "You know, it's the funniest thing. Two days ago a friend gave me this cross on my lapel. Yesterday, another friend gave me the doves. Now today, you've given me this card."

All I could think was "Praise the Lord!" With my time in the airport nearly at an end, I shared with her for a few more minutes. She was deeply considering these events and our conversation when I left to catch my flight. There's a quiet in my spirit when I think about this incident that says there just might be a little fudge shop in heaven!

He Never Allows You to Bear More Than You Can Handle

The time was December, 1998. After 25 years of owning my own printing company, economic conditions were forcing me into a merger. I was faced with closing down and liquidating my printing plant in three months, and running the newly merged operation as a vice president. By the end of January, 1999 I still had the remnants of my old company to finalize out of existence and the newly merged company was fending off a union challenge. On top of all that, I learned the roots of the new company were steeped in illegal and immoral soil. To cap things off, Deborah was diagnosed with two different types of breast cancer, ranked between stages 2 and 3.

The good news was that Jesus' love for us had not changed one dot and He was still sitting on His throne. He led us as we sifted through the medical maze of options and opinions. Self education and care management were major keys, but all were thoroughly marinated in prayer. The complexity of navigating the medical system mandates letting God lead you for the best chance of success.

During the next 16 months, Deborah endured 10 surgeries both major and minor, 8 debilitating chemo treatments and seven weeks of radiation therapy. Her care was the primary element in our family life. While Jesse was still not yet two years old and in diapers, Sara was not yet five years old but was attending Christian pre-school three days a week. We stripped everything possible out of our lives to free up dollars and time. As we were doing all we could, God stepped up to the plate and provided the rest. We had maintained a close personal relationship with Him, through Jesus Christ, our Lord and Savior. The Holy Spirit, living in our hearts, was also a key to this communion. He gave us His Word to claim and rest in, he gave us supportive family, and he gave us a Home Fellowship of Christian believers who showed us by their actions "what Jesus would do."

I would be remiss if I did not include a note of thanks to those God used to bless us. Our home fellowship blessings came from Dave and Cheryl, Doug and Mary, Linda and Mike, Dave and Christine, and others. A local Messianic synagogue in Yardley also adopted our family as a regular care ministry. The Lord provided a retired dentist friend, Barry, who gave us his services for child care and conversation, two days a week, for nearly two full years. God also sent us a sweet grandmom substitute, Hildi, who cared for the children, and often for Deborah, two days a week. Coincidentally, Hildi and my father were from the same town in Germany. We received gifts of money, meals and home services from family and friends. God's provision came in many ways.

One day I was making a sales call on a gymnastics equipment manufacturer. We never did any business together, but Deborah was due to be released from the hospital the next day and the dictates of her surgery required her to maintain a special body angle while she healed. This gentleman gave us a 30° tumbling wedge. It was just the right angle, length and width to provide the best possible positioning and comfort for her in bed. The list of blessings and sources was staggering.

After the first few months – and until this very day – God gave Deborah a cancer-care ministry. A steady flow of people have sought her out. Some have come through our church relationships, some from other churches, some from life experiences and some from Fox Chase Cancer Center itself. It is true that "all things happen for the good, for those who love God and are called according to His purposes." Vicki is just one of those to whom our family ministered, and this is her love story.

Vicki's diagnosis was similar to Deborah's, with multiple types of breast cancer that had spread far into the lymph nodes. Her initial surgery followed Deborah's by about six months. Deborah and Vicki had spoken on the telephone once or twice, but had never met. Vicki was awaiting a date for her surgery, while Deborah was awaiting a date for her second major procedure. Oddly enough, their next conversation took place when they awakened from anesthesia as room mates at Fox Chase!

If you haven't figured it out by now, there are NO coincidences. Vicki had little family, and none close-by. Raised Jewish, she was searching spiritually for the true meaning of life.

During the next few years, Vicki became a very close, beloved friend to all four of us. We saw each other frequently and shared the Gospel with her at every reasonable opportunity, whether in conversation or at special presentations that she and Deborah would attend together. Vicki passed away when her cancer advanced, but she had heard the truth of God and was pondering it. When Deborah visited during her last days, there was a photo of Deborah and our children taped at eye level to the rail of her bed. Vicki's hospital side table held the Bible we had given her and a CD of inspirational scripture readings and songs that had been produced by our church to give comfort to those in sad and difficult circumstances.

We will have to wait to find out what Vicki finally decided. Ultimately, each of us will stand before a righteous God, and only the righteousness we have received in Christ will be good enough to ensure eternal life. Our best efforts will always fall short of the mark. That is His standard, laid out in scripture.

For those of us who by faith are a part of God's family, our obedience will account for our eternal blessings. If you love Jesus, you will do what He directs in all areas of your life. The Bible warns us that a "lukewarm faith" will result in God's spitting us out of His mouth (Rev 3:16). Will your walk be difficult and laden with challenges? Yes, it probably will. Do I understand them all? No, I do not. However, He does not and He will not allow you to bear more than you can handle.   He will be with you every breath of the way, because He loves you.

Jury Duty

I received notice from the county to report for the jury duty pool in the summer of 2000. I had previously served several times, and it had always resulted in sitting in the waiting area for about six hours, then being dismissed. From the beginning, I sensed that this time would be different.

Within the first hour after reporting to the court house, I was selected with many others to be a part of the jury selection in a civil case. All the prospective jurors were asked some basic questions. Through this interview process, 12 jurors were selected and I was one of them.

A woman was suing her periodontist for negligence regarding her oral surgery. She had two dental implants done in the top center of her mouth, teeth numbers 9 and 10. The trial proceeded and we listened to two days of legalese in addition to everything you ever wanted to know (or never wanted to know!) about teeth, gums and oral surgery. Both sides presented their expert witnesses, and, of course, the testimonies of these specialists were often in conflict. The plaintiff's expert witness, a periodontist by training, performed expert witness services as a full time job. His actual dental practice was almost non-existent.

During the course of those first two days of testimony, we 12 jurors listened intently. Well, for the most part that is true. One juror fell asleep the first day and was reprimanded by the judge. On day 2, the same juror fell asleep again! This time the judge told him that if it happened again, he would spend the night in lock-up. We received our guidelines on decision-making from the judge on the third day, retired to the jury room, elected a foreman and got down to deliberation.

Ten votes out of 12 are required for a decision in a civil trial. Before any discussion began, one of my fellow jurors suggested taking a non-binding vote just to "see where we are at this point in time." We all agreed, and the vote was seven for the plaintiff and five for the periodontist. I was one of the five. This was where the real fun began! Of the seven jurors in favor of the plaintiff, the dollar amounts for a punitive award being suggested ranged from $2,000 to $250,000 before considering the pain and suffering coefficient. This coefficient could be many times the actual award figure, if one were granted.

We spent the entire morning going back and forth with review of testimonies, comments, questions and opinions of each juror. Some of these were what I'd consider classics. For example: "He's a doctor and he has plenty of money." Or: "The insurance company is going to pay for it, so what's the big deal?" And: "I really hate going to the dentist." One of the strong arguments against the plaintiff was that she had clearly lied on two or three issues. We five believed that meant she was probably lying about other things as well. The other seven jurors agreed she had lied, but excused it with the attitude that "everybody lies sometimes." Amazingly to me, the fellow who had fallen asleep twice was the proponent of the $250,000 award. After some questioning of his basis for proposing that number, he shared his feeling of kinship for the plaintiff because she was a union worker. The five of us who were siding with periodontist were shocked. Our intent was to bring about justice, based upon the facts presented in the trial. To us, personal opinions and agendas had no place here. We were deadlocked.

The judge called us back into the courtroom and scolded us. We were sequestered, and our lunch was sent into us. During the course of the afternoon, emotions heated up as everyone grew weary of the same commentary and discussion. Someone suggested a minor settlement for the plaintiff as a basis for breaking the deadlock. The question then became what would be the least amount acceptable. I said not even one dollar should be awarded. My reasoning, which I voiced, was that if I ever saw this man (the periodontist) on the street I would be totally ashamed of myself as I looked him in the eyes.

It was now late afternoon and the lady sitting to my right poured herself a glass of water from a lidded brown plastic pitcher. As she finished pouring, I asked her to pass it to me. "It's empty," she said. "I'll get the bailiff to bring us some more." I could hardly believe the next words out of my mouth: "That's not necessary. God will supply all my needs through Christ Jesus," I said as I placed my hand on the pitcher. I picked it up and poured myself a full glass of water! Her jaw dropped. "How did you do that?" she asked. "It wasn't me," I replied, "It was Jesus." Three or four others sitting nearby clearly saw and heard the event. Even this miracle didn't change a single vote, so the foreman again notified the judge that we were hopelessly deadlocked.

Without our knowing any of the specifics, both the defendant and the plaintiff agreed to a settlement based on the jury's actual vote total. The dollar amount would change depending on how many jurors voted in favor of the plaintiff or defendant. Neither party was aware of how the jury's vote was split. The judge recalled us to the jury box and we voted, one at a time. The vote was still seven to five, and as I looked over at the doctor, he was smiling from ear to ear. The judge thanked the jury and dismissed us as they were finalizing the court's ruling.

I went back to the jury room with the other jurors, retrieved my coat and exited down the back stairs. As I walked around the building to reach the parking lot, guess who crossed my path. It was the periodontist. I stopped, and he looked me right in the eyes and said "Thank you!"

Another day is coming when the Judge will again look me in the eyes. I am totally at peace as to what He will say – "Well done, my good and faithful child." This won't be because I had led a perfect or anywhere near perfect life. It will be because I have allowed Jesus to be Lord of my life and my personal Savior.

I Must Do a Better Job of Loving My Wife

In September of 2000, I was blessed with the opportunity to attend the International Conference of the Fellowship of Companies for Christ. This was a much- needed break for me from my care-provider status of the previous one and a half years. The teaching, sharing and fellowship at these conferences is always excellent, and this one was no exception. Bruce Wilkinson was the main speaker, and the secondary speakers were of the same high caliber.

While Bruce was speaking on the second day of the conference, my attention turned to a man and his wife who walked into the session a few minutes late. As they came down the aisle and passed me, I sensed the Holy Spirit had given me an assignment. I was to go to this man and give him a message. Now, I'd never seen this man before in my life! I didn't know his name or anything about him. The message was: "You need to do a better job of loving your wife."

Well, there was no way I wanted to deliver this message! All during Bruce's teaching, I could not shake this thought, and prayed hard.   At a 30 minute break, I called Deborah and confessed to her that I needed to do a better job of loving her. I asked for forgiveness in specific areas of our life together, and then shared with her what I felt the Holy Spirit was asking me to do. She prayed, and told me I should go ahead and deliver the message.

Following our conversation, I sought out this man, introduced myself to him and engaged him in light conversation.   Finally, I asked if I could share something personal about him that I believed the Holy Spirit was telling me. He seemed surprised, and said "Sure!" in a very friendly manner.   I proceeded. "Look," I said. "There is no easy way for me to say this. I believe that God wants you to do a better job of loving your wife. I was so convinced of this that before talking to you, I called my own wife and had the same conversation." Well, he could hardly believe what he was hearing from me. In a polite manner, he thanked me and went on to explain that he and his wife loved each other and their relationship was OK. Because I had no specifics, he again thanked me tepidly and we re-entered the main conference hall for the next session.

Bruce took the podium for part three of his topic. He began to speak, but about two or three minutes into his presentation he put his outline down on the podium. He stood quietly for a minute, apparently doing nothing. Finally, he shook his head a few times and said, "I really don't like it when God does this to me. However, I have to be obedient. Forget the topic for this session, because God just gave me a new topic. First, I'm going to talk to you men – myself included – about how we need to do a better job of loving our wives." He then went on to share about a number of issues.

Especially guilty are business owners, pastors and those who are employed as full time ministry staff, he noted, sharing how we fall into these pits and how we can prevent it from happening again. He then had an altar call for men who were guilty of this sin, had not repented, and needed to do so.

I was blown away by what was taking place. I personally missed walking that aisle by a half hour. However, leading the charge to the altar was the man to whom I had spoken earlier. Approximately half of the men in that room went to the altar that day.

Then Bruce spoke to the wives in the room regarding the need for forgiveness in their hearts concerning their husbands. He elaborated on this topic and again had an altar call. The wife of my "friend" went forward, along with 3/4 of the women in the room. The tissues were flying.

As we broke the session for lunch, I sought out Bruce and shared with him that feeling you get when God wants you to be a part of coloring way, *way*, outside the lines. My calling, one hour before his, was a confirmation to him just as his was to me.

How do you know that it really *IS* God placing a thought or words in your heart?

The answer is, you don't. There are some guidelines for discernment, however.

1. Pray and seek counsel in the time frame allowed.
2. Question whether it conforms to Scripture.

3. Ask whether you stand to gain personally from it. If the answer is yes, be extra cautious.

4. When you just can't let go of the thought, ask Jesus for help and call out His name repeatedly.

When all lights are green, step out in faith and lovingly share the words.

Remember, after 40 years in the wilderness, the River Jordan stood between the nation of Israel and the Promised Land. The river was at flood stage, and appeared dangerous to cross. It wasn't until the priests (you and I in this situation) put their feet into the water that God stopped the water and they were able to enter into the Promised Land.

God Goes to Work with You

As part of my marketing plan for my business, I prayerfully entered into a networking organization. Simply stated, my job is to steer business to others in the group and their job is to steer work to me. I had learned some years before that God works in all circumstances.

From October, 2003 to October, 2005 I actively networked with the group. A portion of this activity was dedicated to building one-on-one relationships. As God opened doors of opportunity, I shared what God had done for me.

One such occasion occurred with a new friend, Andy. Andy came from a traditional religious background. He saw through the falsehood there, and basically was doing his own thing. He was a good guy. That should be OK with God, right: One day, Andy and I had a chance to have lunch together. I shared my faith with him at length. He was resistant. However, he did confide that two other people were telling him the exact same things I was saying. Gee, what a coincidence.

We had lunch again a few months later. After considerable discussion I asked him to tell me what, in his view, was the downside of what I was proposing to him. He answered concisely: "I don't want to look foolish." He also understood the downside of rejecting my proposal – eternal separation from God in a place of continual suffering. Yet, he stood fast. About a month later, on Easter Sunday morning while sitting by himself before church services began, the Holy Spirit touched Andy's heart. In the privacy of that quiet moment, his name was inscribed in the Lamb's Book of Life.

The very next week, I was having lunch at my home with another friend from the group, Mark. We sat at our kitchen table to discuss his printing needs and have a sandwich. In the course of conversation, he asked if I had seen the movie *The Passion of the Christ*. My wife and I were planning to see it that weekend and he was doing the same. I asked his permission to ask him a question. He agreed, so I proceeded with "Who do you think Jesus is?" "Good question," he responded. "Well, I think Jesus is the Son of God," he added. I agreed with him and went on to point something out. "The Bible tells us that Jesus had numerous encounters with Satan and his henchmen," I said. "On every occasion, they addressed Jesus in a similar way and were always very respectful to Him. So now we come to the core question: If our adversaries agree that Jesus is the Son of God, mustn't there be something more that defines being a Christian?

Indeed, there is," I continued. "It is in my believing that I am a sinner and Jesus died for me, as payment for my sins, as my Savior. I accept that free gift and invite Him into my heart to be Lord of my life." Mark thought it over and agreed with me, said a simple prayer, and became part of the family of God.

This was all God's doing: His love, His grace and His omnipotence.   My job was, and remains, to be open and available to His leading.

Saved – A Second Time

We were vacationing in Cape May, NJ in the summer of 2003. We had been blessed with a two-bedroom apartment located just a half-block from the beach. Life was good. When we arrived in that lovely town, we became aware that the National Life Guard Championships were being held in Cape May during the week of our vacation.

As we set up our beach site the first day, there were more than 100 lifeguards within sight. Some portions of the beach and ocean swimming area were cordoned off as venues for the competitions. Shortly after our arrival on the beach, I headed into the water for my first plunge of vacation. The water conditions were pretty rough, so I set out past the breakers and began to body surf, something I have done and enjoyed since I was about six years old. On my third run of the morning, I was atop a wave when a larger cross wave hit me. It caught me from the rear, flipped me, and drove me head-first into the sandy bottom.

My head and neck ached fiercely. I was disoriented and unable to move my limbs properly. My only thought was survival, and I began to crawl along the ocean floor. Thankfully, the Lord was leading me toward the shore rather than out to sea.

As my air began to expire, I reached a spot that was shallow enough for me to lift my head and get a breath. Still unable to stand, I crawled out of the ocean on all fours. I remained there at the water's edge for what seemed like five minutes. Finally, with a severe head and neck ache, I was able to shakily stand and make my way back to our chairs. Through all of this, no one offered so much as one word of assistance. It was as if I was invisible. Deborah's eyes were keening affixed –as they should have been – on our two young kids and a friend of our daughter's who had joined us for the week.

I told Deborah about the experience and spent the next few hours physically regrouping. As time went by, my condition continued to improve ever-so-slightly and I opted not to seek medical assistance. After all, we were on vacation! I did spend ample time reviewing the events with God. Because I wasn't hot-dogging, I felt peace that I hadn't brought this upon myself by acting foolishly. I also found great solace in the fact that I hadn't died and that my condition was slowly improving. The remainder of the week was uneventful other than that a good time was had by all.

When we returned home, I went to see a friend who is a sports medicine doctor and explained the events to him. He took x-rays and asked lots of questions regarding my symptoms. Finally, he gave me his summary and directives for treatment. "You were fortunate not to die on the spot," he said. "In addition, it's a miracle you are functioning and were able to walk in here today." I had broken my C-6 vertebra and had moderate spinal compression. This essentially is the same injury that paralyzed the actor Christopher Reeve as the result of a horse riding accident. Once again, I knew that God's hand was upon me in a big-time way.

My treatments have helped, but my sports career is over. Mild exercise is OK, as long as there are no activities that raise my arms above shoulder-level or cause contact. I am now relegated to walking, bicycling and swimming. Life is extremely fragile.

In one brief moment, I came close to being paralyzed or dead. It is only by God's grace that I was spared. I know that all things happened for the good for those who love God and are called according to His purpose. My being saved meant to me that God had other purposes for me. It is the desire of my heart to be faithful to His plan for me. How about you? Where are you today? I can tell you quite candidly that I don't have those answers for you. However, as sure as you are that you are reading these words, He does.

Destination Wedding

My niece, Nikki, was married in the summer of 2004. Weddings are nearly always a great time. It's joyous moment. Family and friends gather for hugs, kisses, dancing, food, drink and a good ol' get together. My niece and her fiancé, however, decided to have their wedding at a great resort on the island of St. Lucia. For us, this decision represented two challenges: The resort did not allow children and the cost of this trip was totally out of our budget. But we went to prayer over our decision whether or not to attend, and were confident that the Lord said "Go." Friends kindly cared for our children, and away we went.

It was almost like a second honeymoon for us. The resort was everything we could have hoped for, with beautiful scenery and wonderful amenities. Unfortunately, I had been misinformed by my travel agent concerning the need for slacks. I took none, and this was a no-no at this upscale establishment. We spent our first morning in town, shopping for pants. As we made our first purchase, I left the cashier a "thank you" witnessing card. While we were in the second store, a woman came up to us and asked if I had any more of those cards. Her co-worker had showed her the one I'd left at the previous shop, and they both loved it. She wanted to have one for herself. At that point, we felt a confirmation of the hand of God on our trip.

The wedding service was very beautiful. The resort provided most of the services with no options. Here again, all were blessed by the man officiating. His words were biblical and filled with God's point of view as illustrated in scripture.

In addition to all of the normal, fun activities like swimming, snorkeling, sailing, touring and more that one would expect at a Caribbean resort, each person received a daily spa treatment of some sort. The only word to describe this, at least to me, is WOW!

The wedding party consisted of only 18 people, so we were able to develop a closeness with every person attending in a way that normally would not be possible.

Another blessing was that I was able to resume pursuing an old sport of mine, scuba diving. I had not been diving for about 15 years, so after taking a pool test, a snorkel test and a shallow water dive, I anxiously awaited two deep dives scheduled for the next morning. We set out early in the morning, numbering two divers and two instructors. That limited number is the best thing. As we approached the first dive site, the conversation ran to whether there was a chance of rain. The other diver said "Only God knows the answer to that question," with which we all agreed. I kept the conversation going with further comments about God. The head instructor picked up on this the most. She and I mostly dialogued while the other two listened. After we spoke for a few minutes, she wanted me to know that her uncle was an evangelical pastor and

"I've heard it all before." I asked for permission to ask a few questions, and she agreed. "I understand that you have heard it all before," I said. "You and I both understand that even good divers, following all the rules, sometimes have fatal accidents. If that happens to you today, what is your plan?"

She was speechless. "Would you like to have a plan before we begin our dive?" I continued. She began to cry. I held her hands and said "Let's pray." She prayed with me at the back of the boat and opened her heart to Jesus. I tell you, that was the greatest day of diving I'd had in all of the 36 years I'd been doing it! On our way back to the marina, we made plans for her to join Deborah and me for dinner. As I shared this with Deborah upon returning, we were on Cloud Nine. Halleluiah, praise God, He is so good.

When dinner time came, she didn't show. We waited, prayed, waited, and then had our dinner. This was our last night in St. Lucia. Uncertainty about what was happening filled our thoughts, but we rested in the fact that God was in control and that was fine. In the morning, as we were packing, I returned some towels and happened to cross paths with the diving instructor just as she was coming to work. She ran up and hugged and kissed me! "Praise the Lord," she said. "I apologize for standing you guys up for dinner last night. However, I was exhausted and there was one thing I just had to do. I called my boyfriend and told him I had to see him right away. When he arrived, I told him that although I cared for him very much, I was saying good-bye. I shared my new faith with him and explained I could no longer live the lifestyle I was living. I am walking down a new path, and so I must say good-bye," she continued. "He responded by saying 'Whatever path you are walking, I want to walk it with you." The two of them prayed together, and he committed his life to the Lord.

When I related all of this back in the room, Deborah and I were again moved to tears by how good our God is. We had been given a small taste of heaven. There really are not words to describe His goodness. Thank you, Father; thank you, Jesus and thank you, Holy Spirit.

The E-Mail from Nowhere

In December, 2006 I received an e-mail from a woman named Sandy _____ _____. She was looking for me, and had done a Google search that led her to our e-mail address. Her question was a simple one: "Are you the guy who used to own a printing company in Southampton?" Due to the possibilities of viruses and other mal-ware invading our computers, I am very wary of strange e-mails. However, there were no attachments and she already had my address.

With some hesitation, I responded that I was the same fellow. You see, I know a number of people with similar names. I just didn't recognize the full name she had given me or the address.

Her reply arrived a few days later. "My mother is Marilyn," she wrote. Marilyn was my bookkeeper for a number of years, and Marilyn and Sandy would occasionally clean my townhouse. We had dinner a few times, or just hung out together.

"I am married, now," she wrote, "and that's my new name. You have been on my heart for awhile. I just wanted to tell you how much you have blessed me from my youth. My life and faith today are directly related to God's working through you."

"Blown away" is the only way I could describe my feelings.

I had not seen Sandy in 20 years! My memories were all very favorable, but contact with her had been very minimal.

This all too clearly reminds me of the far-reaching depth of the ministry we have in the name of Jesus. My prayer is to have His eyes, so I can see more deeply the Reality of what I am about.

Two Miracles in One Week

Early in 2007 we forgot to pay our quarterly business taxes. It was a clear-cut case of OOPS. As you might expect, we received a computerized message from the IRS. What had been a $9,000.00 deposit-due now had $900.00 in penalties and $90.00 in interest due as well. Because we were guilty as charged, we paid Caesar. Along with the check, our accountant included a letter stating the item simply had fallen through the cracks due to a paperwork filing error. Although we were guilty, we requested grace. About a month later we received their response: As a one-time dispensation, we would be refunded the $990.00, and in addition, we were to receive interest of $3.70 on our payment. How do you spell "Praise the Lord?"

The same week we received the grace refund from the IRS, our son's foot received God's healing grace. Jesse had injured his foot at school six weeks earlier. After x-rays, we had been told by the emergency room physician that no bones were broken and that it was a sprain. Treatment was to ice it, elevate and rest it as much as possible, and it "should be better in two to three weeks." The swelling did, indeed, disappear fairly quickly but the pain did not.

After three weeks we consulted an orthopedic surgeon, who x-rayed it again, looking for a hairline fracture. There was none visible. This doctor also suggested waiting for two weeks. "If the pain is not significantly improved, then he may have a LisFranc sprain," he said. An injury like that could take up to a year to heal and rehab properly, but the condition can only be determined through an MRI. We waited the two weeks, and one more besides. Still the pain persisted. We had the referral for the MRI in hand, but felt led to hold a private healing service for Jesse in our home before proceeding further medically.

In the quiet of our living room, Dr. Jesus made a house call and Jesse's foot was healed. He was back on the soccer field the following week. God is so good. Where would we be without him?

Seasons of Warfare

When I wake up in the morning, my first thoughts concern whether I should actually get out of bed, or what today's schedule holds for me. As I settle into my daily routine, my natural thoughts are centered on the physical interactions of my life. I fully understand that each of these thoughts and actions are natural and fine in basic content. However, there is a larger reality that is just as present. That reality is that we are at war. War may manifest itself in our fight against extremists. Sometimes nations fight over territory, natural resources or for personal freedoms. Again, these are all in the physical realm. Although not directly visible to the naked eye, we also are very much at war on a spiritual level. Whether you agree or not, like it or not, our spiritual lives and physical lives are linked. They are linked today and through eternity.

With this thought in mind, please remember that I have written this book so that you may be blessed by God. God's blessings come in unusual ways. His thoughts are not my thoughts and His ways are not my ways. If at any time while you were reading this book, you felt upset or if you got your feathers ruffled, please remember my intentions. My interest is for you to be blessed spiritually.

So what do you do when you are angered, confronted by others or just uncomfortable regarding a real life situation? Remember, there is a spiritual war taking place for the lordship of your heart. On one side is a holy and perfect God. On the other is our spiritual adversary in combination with our deceiving hearts. Yes, my heart (and yours) is deceitful above all things (Jeremiah 17:9). These are two reasons for the heat of your confrontation:

Reason 1 – You are doing the right thing according to God's plan, and so are under attack by the evil one, aided by your own sin nature. Well, what is the right thing according to God? It is the Word of God, the Bible, from Genesis to Revelation. Add nothing to this and take nothing away. God means what He says and says what He means. The Spirit of God will also aid us. Be open and obedient. Also remember, the Word of God and the Spirit of God are in perfect oneness (*echaud*). So when the heat is turned up, seek the Lord (His Word and Spirit) and actively apply His principles to your situation. Seeking godly counsel is an excellent confirmation step after you have applied step one. Then, walk obediently in faith. He will do the rest.

Reason 2 – You are NOT doing the right thing according to God's plan and you are under the heart conviction of the Holy Spirit. Yes, God is actually standing at the door to your heart and knocking. Sometimes, the knock is loud. But if you choose to walk in self-pride and arrogance, rejecting His lordship, you can sufficiently callous your heart. Over time, you will become less and less sensitive to His truth and His love. Only you can open that door.

Some say God's way is "not fair." I say, what gives me the right to have a personal relationship with a righteous and holy God for eternity? I am thankful that he has given me *any* way to have that blessing, when I clearly do not deserve it. So here you are. Ask this question: "Dear Lord, in the name of Jesus (Yeshua), is it true or is it not true?"

I have found the answers for myself, as each one of us must do. If you want to walk closer with God, then from your heart say a prayer like this, right where you are:

"Dear heavenly Father, in the name of Jesus (Yeshua), I want to live my life with you as my Lord, Savior and best friend. I know I am a sinner and that sin separates me from you. However, I accept the free gift of salvation you have provided for me. The shed blood of Christ, my Messiah, cleanses me of all my sins past, present and future. I desire your Lordship in my life from this moment forward. Thank you."

Now, go and read your Bible (even for five minutes!) every day, pray in the name of Jesus (Yeshua), and He will do the rest.

Be blessed.

Seasons of Waiting

I am, by nature, someone who does not like to wait. It's OK if I take my good old time making my mind up. But once I have decided something, push-button speed is not too soon! I think most of us are like this — perhaps not as bad as I am, but not that much better.

Yet, God says His ways are not my ways. Mary was encouraged just to sit at the feet of Jesus as opposed to Martha, who was scurrying around, "doing all the work," when Jesus visited their home.

A season of waiting affords us the luxury of being still. Let's not squander it with something silly like worry. It is a time to draw more closely to Jesus, which is something we all need. When I draw near to Him, He will draw near to me. It affords each of us the opportunity to hear God better by being more committed to our quiet time, prayer time and Bible studies. We can more fully internalize our Lord in every aspect of life itself. It's a time to grow in thankfulness and forgiveness. Seasons of waiting give me (and you) a chance to adjust to His game plan and schedule for our lives.

It is also a season in which God does His thing. He works

in the hearts and minds of other people as well as through events, meetings, and other things. It's exhilarating just to relax and let God be God. There is so much peace to be found in the truth that "I (Stan) make a really lousy Holy Spirit." He can and will do the job perfectly and for free.

When I make my heart available to God, whatever follows is just flat-out beautiful. So Father, Jesus and Holy Spirit, I recommit my life to You. Whatever needs to be done in my life, just do it. If I can be used in some way to assist, I am available. If it takes 5 minutes or 50 years, that's OK. I love You.

Thanks for being my best friend.

Stan